HI-TECH JOBS WITHOUT COLLEGE

BE A WEB DESIGNER

by Kari Cornell

BrightPoint Press

San Diego, CA

Bri[illegible]htPoint Press

an imprint of ReferencePoint Pr[illegible]s, Inc.
Printed in the United States

For more information, contact:
BrightPoint Press
PO Box 27779
San Diego, CA 92198
www.BrightPointPress.com

LIBRARY O[illegible]ONGRESS CATALOGING-IN-PUBLICATION DATA

Names: Cornell, Kari A., [illegible]hor.
Title: Be a web designer [illegible] Kari Cornell.
Description: San Diego, [illegible] BrightPoint Press, [2025] | Series: Hi-tech jobs without college | Includes bibliographica[illegible]ferences and index. | Audience: Grades 7-9
Identifiers: LCCN 20240[illegible]83 (print) | LCCN 2024001084 (eBook) | ISBN 9781678209445 (hardcover) | ISBN 978[illegible]8209452 (eBook)
Subjects: LCSH: Web si[illegible]evelopment industry--Vocational guidance--Juvenile literature.
Classification: LCC HD9[illegible].82.A2 C67 2025 (print) | LCC HD9696.82.A2 (eBook) | DDC 006.7023--dc23/eng/[illegible]40205
LC record available at h[illegible]://lccn.loc.gov/2024001083
LC eBook record availa[illegible]at https://lccn.loc.gov/2024001084

CONTENTS

AT A GLANCE

- Web designers make websites easy to use so people can find what they need quickly. They must think about user experience (UX).

- A domain name is an address on the web. Web designers must register domain names to prevent other companies or people from using them.

- Web designers test websites to make sure they work on different devices. A website designed for a computer screen may not work as well on a smartphone.

- The content of a website is written using HyperText Markup Language (HTML). Another computer language, Cascading Style Sheets (CSS), adds style to a website, including colors and fonts.

- People can go through short, intense programs to learn about web design. These are known as boot camp programs.
- Both beginners and professionals can earn certificates to learn new programs and techniques.
- Advancing technologies mean the web design field is always changing. Artificial intelligence (AI) systems may help make websites more accessible by turning images into written or spoken language.

A WEB DESIGNER'S DAY

Web designer Kay Cinho doesn't like mornings. But coffee helps. He checks his schedule. He has a meeting with a client about a website problem. Then he will meet with a barbershop owner who wants to start a website. This meeting is very important. Cinho will ask lots of questions. He will explain his design process. He will show examples of sites he's designed. What he learns will shape

Meetings with clients may happen in person, over the phone, or on video calls.

The basic layout of a website is figured out early in the web design process.

the rest of the project. Both meetings go well. Cinho explained, "I managed to find a solution for my client, and the barbershop may well become a new client."[1]

Back at his office, Cinho studies notes from another client meeting. He begins to design a wireframe. This is a basic plan for a website's layout. He uses fake text instead of real content. But the wireframe shows the client how the site will look. The client must approve it before Cinho designs the site.

Next Cinho creates a mood board. This is a page filled with images, colors, and fonts. The mood board shows how the final design will feel. He considers the client's goals and comes up with a plan. Then the designing begins. He uses the wireframe as a map to create the website.

Web design is not easy. But Cinho likes having a chance to express his creativity. He said, "I'm so passionate about web design [. . .] that even when the days are hard, I always remember the chance I have, this freedom I have."[2]

Whenever people browse the web on their phones, they are seeing the work of web designers.

WHAT DOES A WEB DESIGNER DO?

Web designers like Cinho lay out websites. They arrange images, text, and other features that explain the client's business goals. Designers arrange these elements to make the site look good. They add menus. These features organize information for users.

Web designers make websites easy to use. Their work helps people find what they need quickly. This is called *user experience* (*UX*). Millions of people see the work of web designers every day.

CHAPTER ONE

EXPLORING WEB DESIGN

There is more to web design than just making websites look good. People are using the internet more than ever before. They shop for groceries and clothes online. People buy tickets to shows. They go online to schedule appointments. Web designers help make all of this possible.

People decide which companies to work with based on their websites. This means websites must look professional.

Web design is often a collaborative process.

If a website is hard to use, customers may visit a competitor's site. Typos or sloppy design will make customers look elsewhere. A simple, well-designed site brings in more customers. It makes the company look good.

Graphic designers develop a knowledge of which colors go well together.

WHAT IS WEB DESIGN?

Web designers help shape their clients' public image. They meet with clients to learn about the clients' projects. Web designers ask questions and plan the overall look of the site. They design sample pages to show the client.

Designers carefully choose the colors, fonts, and graphics used on websites. They select photos and videos. Designers meet with writers to talk about the content. They bring in graphic designers to create visual elements. And they arrange the text and images to create the user interface. This is what people see on the screen when they go to a website. If web designers have done their job well, people can easily **navigate** the site. Web designer Martin LeBlanc put it this way: "A user interface is like a joke. If you have to explain it, it's not that good."[3]

Web designers also think about how the site will be used. Different types of websites do different things. Companies such as Amazon and Nike sell products. They have online stores that can accept payments. Personal websites or blogs need to be well organized so users can find what they're looking for. Web designs for small businesses should look and feel like the company they represent.

BEHIND THE SCENES

Web designers may have other tasks as well. Some designers register web domains. A web domain is an address on the web. A memorable or catchy domain can help

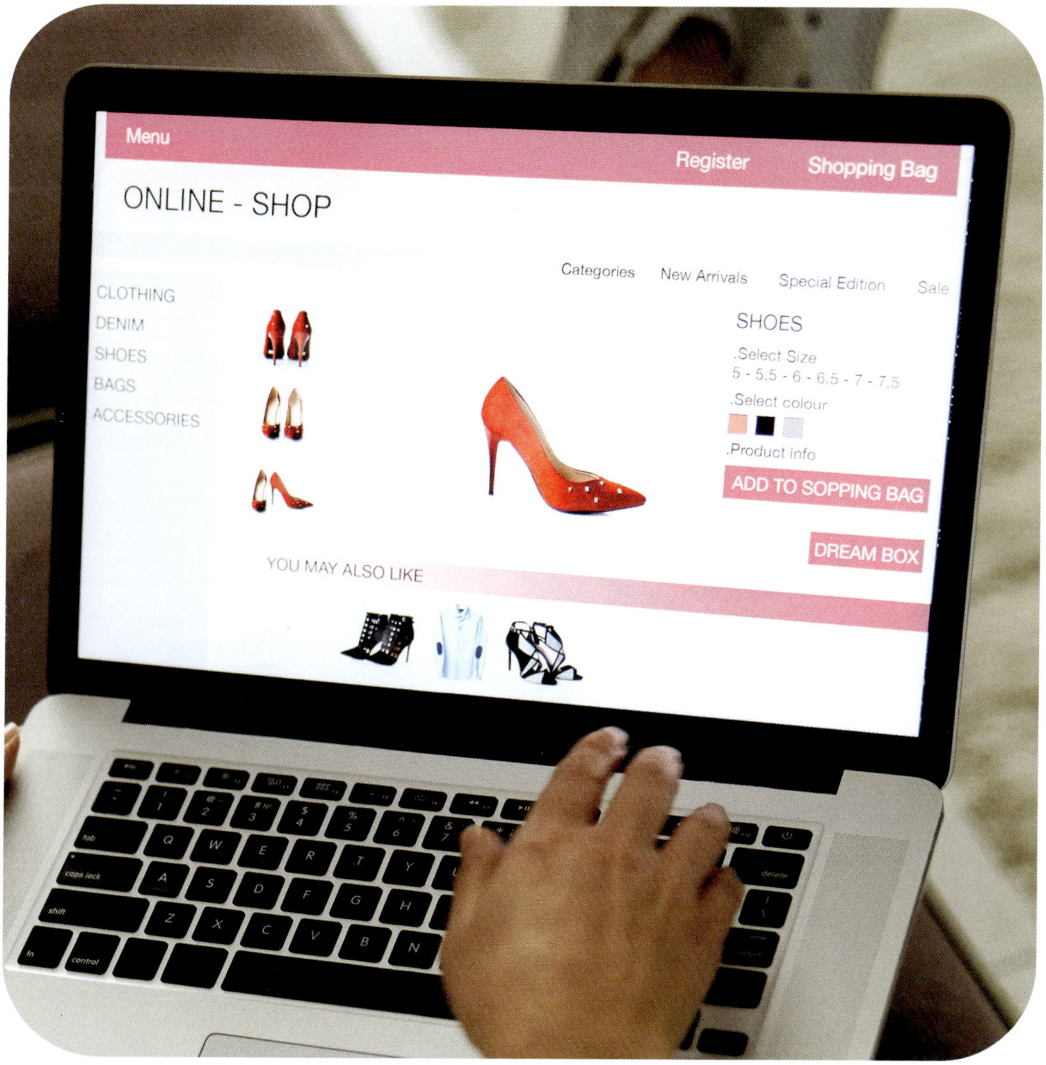

Websites for specific purposes, such as shopping, may need unique features.

people find a website. Registering a domain name prevents other companies from using the same name. Web designers may also keep track of how many people visit

Metrics give web designers and their clients insight into how visitors are using a website.

the site. And they may check to see how many visitors buy something or sign up for mailing lists. These numbers are examples of metrics. Metrics can help web designers improve the site and increase visitors.

Some web designers also test websites. They make sure websites work on different devices. A website designed for a laptop may not work as well on a phone. The smaller screen means web pages need to be created with responsive design. This allows pages to smartly **scale** for any size of device. Designers may also try to make pages load faster. For example, they can have the page load images only when a user scrolls down to them. Web designers may also update websites when clients request changes.

WHAT SKILLS ARE NEEDED?

Good web designers have both artistic and technical skills. They need an eye for design. They should know what colors work together. They should be able to balance elements in a layout. Web designers should also know how to draw and use **typography**. A creative design can make a website stand out.

Web designers must know design programs like Adobe Illustrator and Photoshop. They also need to know website-building programs such as Webflow. They should know wireframe programs such as Figma. Knowing how to use **animation** programs such as Motion and After Effects is helpful too. Designers should also learn HTML and CSS. HTML is HyperText Markup Language. It is used to write the structure and content of a web page. CSS stands for Cascading Style Sheets. It is used to add style to a page, including colors and fonts.

Adobe Photoshop is often used to edit images for the web.

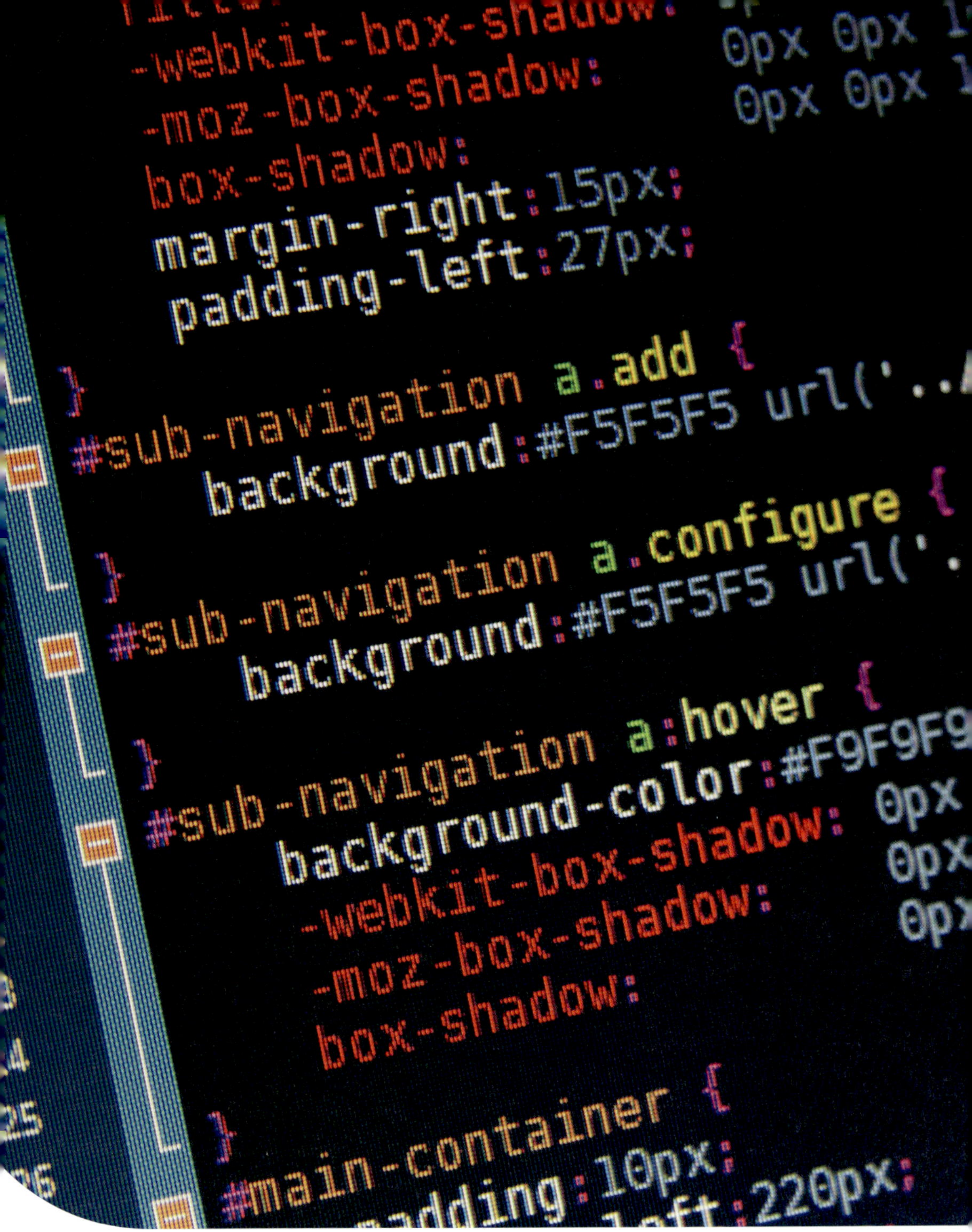

Knowing how to read HTML and CSS helps web designers know why a web page looks the way it does.

Designers must also be able to collaborate. They will work with writers, graphic designers, and web developers. Good communication skills are a must. Designers meet with a lot of clients. They must be able to explain ideas clearly. Web designers must also be able to meet and manage deadlines.

Web Designer vs. Web Developer

Web developers write the programming code that makes a website work. For example, a web developer might create a tool that lets users search a social media website. Web designers make websites look good. They also think about how easy the site is to use. For example, a web designer might decide how a user's profile page looks on a social media website.

CHAPTER TWO

TRAINING FOR THE JOB

There are many ways to become a web designer. But there is a common set of coding and design skills that web designers need. How people gain these skills is up to them.

Different paths might include coding boot camps or online classes. There are also certification programs. Many web designers teach themselves. For others, an associate's or bachelor's degree may be the first step.

Many web designers are self-taught.

But web design is a career that does not require a college degree.

Shane Mielke is living proof of this. Mielke is a web designer and creative director. He has designed for SpaceX, Blizzard Entertainment, and Riot Games. He said, "Half of my friends have a design education and the other half are self-taught like myself.

A Bachelor's Degree

A college degree is not necessary for web design. But some web designers do begin with a bachelor's degree. They may get a bachelor of arts or a bachelor of science degree. They may study web design, digital design, or graphic design. Students might take college classes in programming languages, animation, and graphic design tools. They may also learn web design techniques in school.

In the end, all that matters is if your work is any good or not. Some people need the structure and guidance of a formal education. Others are do-it-yourself types who need to move at their own speed and figure things out through trial and error. Neither way is perfect."[4]

WEB DESIGN BOOT CAMPS

With online training, people can gain web design skills on their own time. Many online training **platforms** and universities offer web design boot camps. These are usually 3- to 9-month programs. They teach students essential web design skills.

Many boot camps are offered through online training platforms. Universities around the country offer boot camps as well.

The cost of these programs typically ranges from $9,000 to $14,000.

Boot camp programs begin with the basics. Students learn basic coding concepts, HTML, and the programming language JavaScript. They practice these skills with hands-on projects. Then they move on to more difficult languages such as Python. Students learn CSS and querying languages. Querying languages retrieve data from databases. Classes end with a final project. Students build a website to host their portfolio. Other projects from the boot camp can be used as portfolio pieces.

Placement rates for boot camp students are promising. In 2023 they ranged from 81 to 95 percent, depending on the program. Celeste North completed a boot camp

Web design boot camps can quickly get students up to speed on the important technologies in the field.

called Designlab. She then got a job as a UX designer at a digital banking company. The skills she learned prepared her for the job. “I learned sketching, wireframing, **prototyping**, [. . .] and user flows.

Boot camps can give people the skills they need to land a job in web design.

These are all key skills for my work," she explained.[5]

ONLINE CLASSES AND CERTIFICATION PROGRAMS

Those interested in web design have other options to learn new skills. There are many online courses available. Some focus on Python or HTML. Others teach web design concepts. Students may learn the basics of good design. They learn advanced CSS skills to add style to a website. They may learn how to create animations. These elements will make their site stand out.

Earning a web design certificate is another way to build skills. Designers can earn certificates to demonstrate their knowledge of programs and techniques.

Certificate programs last between a few weeks and a few months. These programs cover topics such as UX, responsive design, and more.

Online tools and tutorials make it possible to learn web design without setting foot in a classroom at all.

SELF-TAUGHT

Many have taught themselves how to create websites. Resources available online make this possible. Designers can visit existing websites and study their HTML and CSS. This helps them learn how to build good sites. They can also discuss web design with others on **forums**. And they can watch how-to videos on specific concepts. Reading books about web development and coding is also a good way to gain knowledge.

There are some advantages for web designers who teach themselves. Shane Mielke explained, "Not knowing some things has helped me be more open to self-growth, experimentation, and just

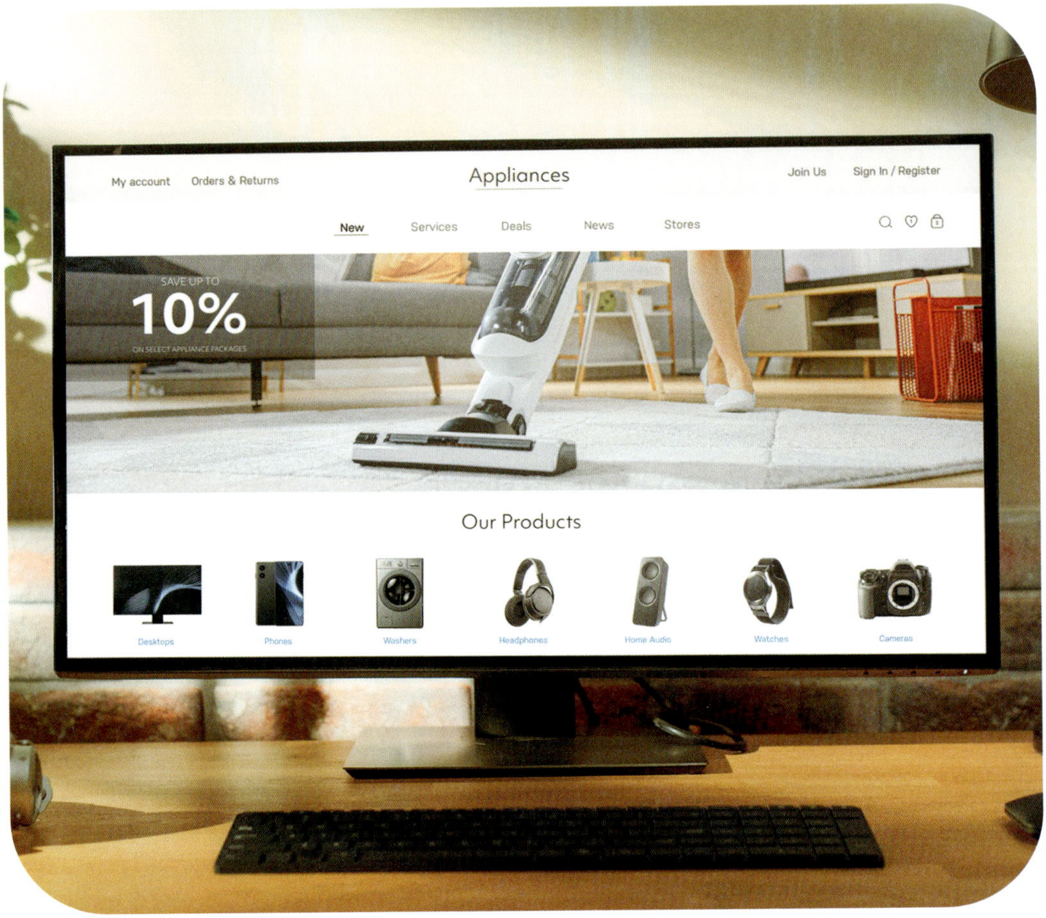

A portfolio should show off work that a web designer is proud of.

having a diverse skill set not limited to any one thing."[6]

BUILDING AN ONLINE PORTFOLIO

All web designers must build a portfolio. They are in the business of creating quality websites. An online portfolio should show their best work.

The portfolio site interface should be user friendly. It should be easy to navigate. The portfolio must include a recent and diverse range of sites. These examples should fit the designer's interests. The portfolio should describe the goal of each project. The designer must explain why it's in the portfolio. Testimonials from clients should be included as well. This is also the place to highlight skills and any certifications or degrees. Designers should include a contact form so employers can reach them.

CHAPTER THREE

WORKING IN THE FIELD

Web designers may work for many different types of companies. Some work for technology companies. Others are hired by publishing companies, advertising firms, or management consulting firms. Many web designers are freelancers. They work for a mix of different clients.

Web designers may work in an office as part of a design team. Offices might have cubicles or an open layout. Some designers

Some web designers collaborate with their fellow workers in an office setting.

may work remotely from home. Others may work at a coworking space. This is a building where workers can rent office space. Designers usually work regular business hours. But they may work extra hours to meet deadlines.

THE DAY BEGINS

Web designers often start their day by checking their email inboxes. A big part of their job is communicating with clients. Emails from clients may be about corrections to current web design projects. They might include information about new projects. Checking their email helps designers plan the rest of their day. Web developer Sam said, "I'll then check for errors and **bug reports** to see if any issues

Checking emails in the morning helps with managing projects and clients.

cropped up while I was gone, and prioritize my to-do list accordingly."[7]

Designers also look at their schedule. It's common for web designers to have client meetings throughout the day. Designer Kay Cinho tries to schedule all meetings for one day of the week. Then he can focus on web design on the other days. Other designers may schedule meetings only during the morning or afternoon. This frees up the rest of the day to work on design projects. But during busy times, no amount of scheduling helps. Web designer Charlotte O'Hara explained, "Some days I have back-to-back

Inspiration from Peers

Web designer Brandon Arnold starts his day by checking in on other leading web designers and developers. He follows the projects they are working on. He reads about what design tools and software they are using. This helps him stay connected and current on industry trends.

client calls or meetings, which means that I just am not productive in other areas of my business. And you know what? That's okay! It all evens out in the end."[8]

MEETINGS

Design projects start with a client meeting. This first meeting is important. It sets the expectations for the project. Good communication makes the design process go smoothly.

Designers ask a lot of questions. The answers help the designer write a client brief. The designer asks the client to give an overview of their organization. They ask about the problem the client wishes to solve through the website. The designer also asks about the audience for the website.

Knowing this helps the designer select colors and set the right tone. The designer also asks the client what features and content the website should have. Finally, they discuss a timeline for the project. This meeting helps the designer understand the client's vision.

Web designers also meet with other people on their team. The team may include a graphic designer and a content specialist. Designers focus on the layout and graphics of the website. Content specialists write the text for the site. A marketing strategist may also be part of the team. They keep track of the budget and timeline for the project. They also find ways to attract people to the site. A web developer anchors the team.

THE WEB DESIGN PROCESS

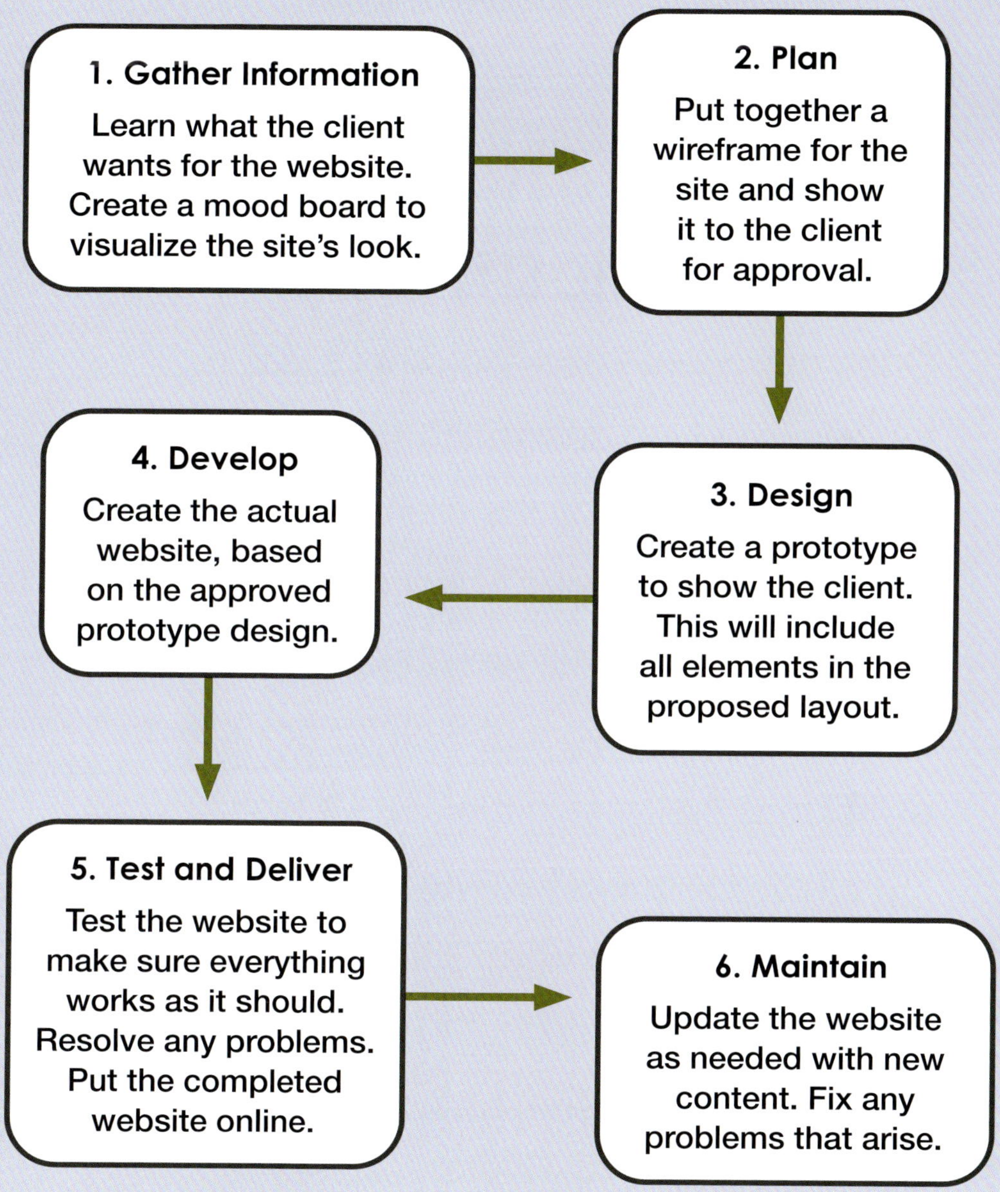

Each web designer creates their own process. But most workflows include the same basic steps.

Developers bring all these ideas together. They write the code to build the website.

DESIGNING THE SITE

Once designers know the client's vision, they are ready to design the website. The first step is reviewing the client brief. Some designers also research design ideas. They look for websites that are similar to the client's vision. Designers look for color and style ideas that match the client's look.

Not all designers follow the same process. In an interview, Shane Mielke explained his approach. "It took years, but I slowly started to see the way I wanted things and no longer had to ask others for advice or look to other websites for inspiration," he said. "Eventually, I reinvented

Client meetings are key for figuring out the vision for a project.

myself and I was no longer just a developer who knew everything about building a site. I evolved into someone with balance as both an artist and a developer."[9]

Designing websites isn't easy. Sometimes designers run into creative roadblocks. They may need to take a break

Group video calls are a great way to share feedback and ideas with remote team members.

to refocus. They may work on another project for a while. This allows designers to do their best work.

At the end of the day, designers may check in with their team. They let the others know what they accomplished. They may give completed projects to the team to review. Then the team makes a plan for the next day.

LOOKING AHEAD

More companies are focusing on their websites. Before people go to a restaurant or store, they will often check out the place online. The website gives a first impression of a business. If the website looks good, people are more likely to do business with the company.

This means the demand for web design is increasing. The career is expected to grow by 15 percent between 2022

Good web design is important for many kinds of businesses.

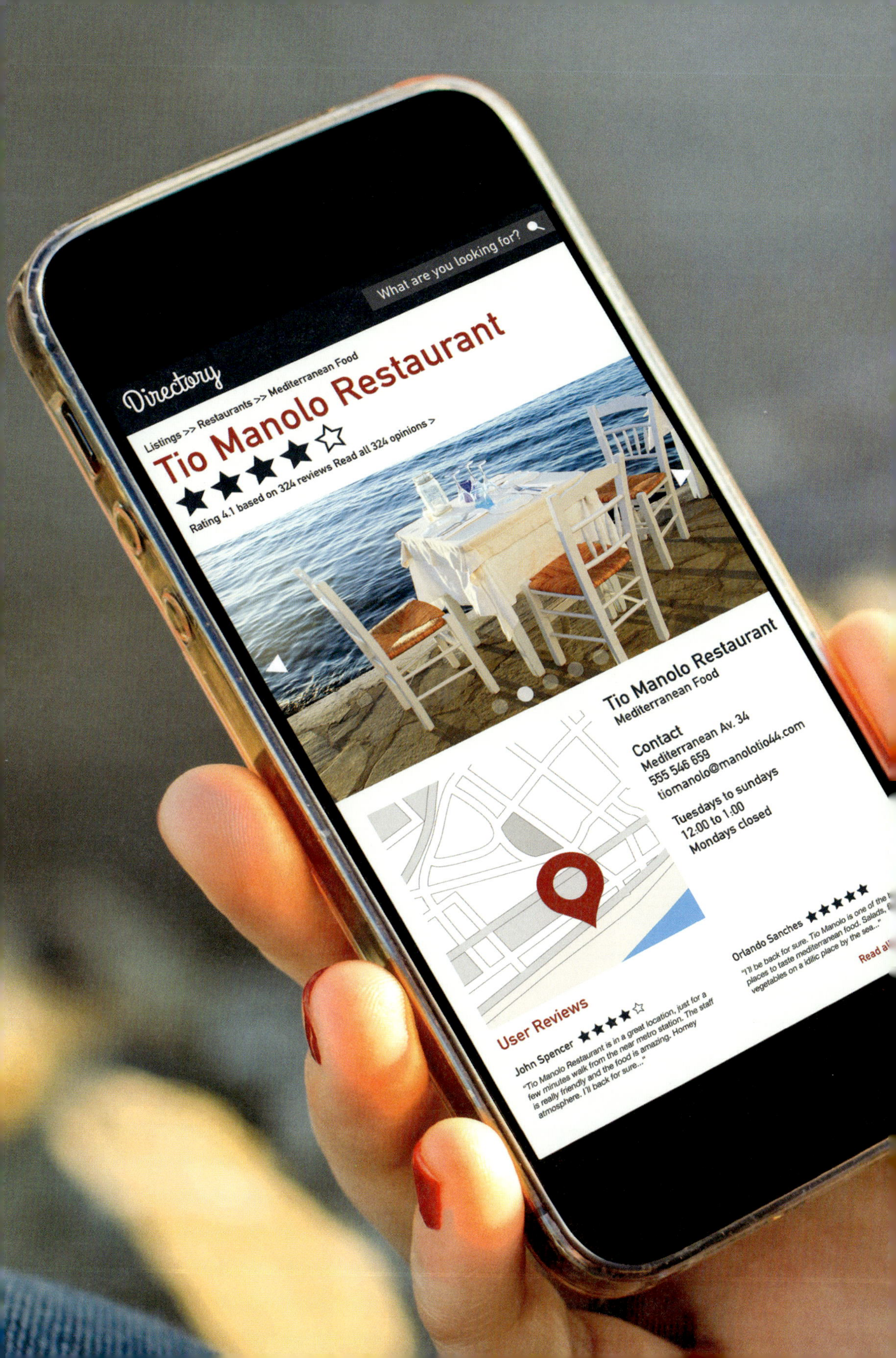

Directory
What are you looking for?
Listings >> Restaurants >> Mediterranean Food
Tio Manolo Restaurant
Rating 4.1 based on 324 reviews Read all 324 opinions >
Tio Manolo Restaurant
Mediterranean Food
Contact
Mediterranean Av. 34
555 546 659
tiomanolo@manolotio44.com
Tuesdays to sundays
12.00 to 1.00
Mondays closed
User Reviews
John Spencer
"Tio Manolo Restaurant is in a great location, just for a few minutes walk from the near metro station. The staff is really friendly and the food is amazing. Homey atmosphere. I'll back for sure..."
Orlando Sanches
"I'll be back for sure. Tio Manolo is one of the
places to taste mediterranean food. Salads,
vegetables on a idilic place by the sea..."

and 2032. Web design is growing much faster than other professions. Experts predict there will be about 18,000 openings over this 10-year period.

WordPress and other tools make building websites more accessible than ever before.

BETTER WEB DESIGN TOOLS

Web design is always adapting to advances in technology. New tools are making it easier to design websites. Craig Frost is a web designer. He explained, "Building websites used to be slow, expensive, and hard to maintain. And it also meant you had to have a lot of skills, a lot of people. Now we're putting the power back into the product builders' hands. Which means you can spend less time maintaining these applications, more on customer needs. Having conversations with them, building things they need."[10]

For example, people can use website platforms such as Weebly and WordPress. These tools allow everyday people to build websites without writing any code. People can focus on how the website looks. The platform takes care of the coding behind the scenes.

Traditionally web designers relied on web developers to help create unique site designs. Designers would gather content and come up with a design. Then they would pass their ideas to a developer to write the code. Thanks to modern tools, this is changing. Experts predict that the jobs of web designer and web developer could combine in the future.

Virtual reality (VR) may become a part of web design. VR provides designers with more tools to enhance the user experience. For example, a person looking at hotels could tour the rooms in VR. Or people could shop for a couch without

VR is affecting many areas of computer technology, including the web.

leaving their home. VR technology could allow them to see how the couch would look in their home.

Designers will be using more animation in websites as well. This is called *motion user interface*. Using moving visuals can make sites easier to navigate. Animated menus make features easier to find. Web designers can also use animation to confirm user actions. This improves the experience for the user.

IMPROVING USER EXPERIENCE

Many people use the web on mobile devices. A 2023 survey found that 60 percent of web traffic came from mobile devices. This is why there's a new focus on mobile-first design. In the past, websites were designed with computer screens in mind. Then sites were adapted for use on mobile devices. But now mobile design is becoming the priority.

Users are also demanding more from websites. They want websites to load faster. Web designers can use a technique called *lazy loading*. Photos on a web page do not load until a user scrolls down

AI and Web Design

Artificial intelligence is improving web design. AI-powered programs can tackle repetitive tasks. They can tag photos and create simple websites. This allows designers to focus on more creative tasks. AI can also be used to predict user behavior. This makes it possible to personalize the user experience.

Web designers have the opportunity to show their work off to millions of people online.

to them. Designers are also using image compression. This decreases the file size of images without affecting their quality. Smaller files load faster.

Artificial intelligence (AI) technology may play a role in future web design. AI systems can create written or spoken descriptions of images. This could be used to improve accessibility for websites. AI could describe images for those who are unable to see them.

Pageless websites are also a rising trend in web design. This means users can simply scroll through one long page. There's no need to click through multiple pages. This may make it easier to navigate the site. But there are some drawbacks. Pageless designs will not work for all types of websites. These can be more complicated to build as well.

These new tools and features make today an exciting time in web design. Web users benefit from improved interfaces. And web designers get to learn new techniques. This allows them to build more engaging sites.

GLOSSARY

animation

a form of art that involves making drawings or images appear to move

bug reports

explanations of errors found in a program or website

forums

websites where people can discuss things

navigate

to move from page to page through a website

platforms

websites that provide a service to users

prototyping

creating an early test version of a website

scale

to adjust the size of something

typography

the style or appearance of text

SOURCE NOTES

INTRODUCTION: A WEB DESIGNER'S DAY

1. Kaycinho: The Digital Alchemist, "Day in the Life Web Designer—Probably Not What You Think," *YouTube*, October 22, 2020. www.youtube.com.

2. Kaycinho: The Digital Alchemist, "Day in the Life Web Designer—Probably Not What You Think."

CHAPTER ONE: EXPLORING WEB DESIGN

3. Quoted in Saadia Minhas, "A User Interface Is Like a Joke," *Medium*, June 20, 2018. https://uxdesign.cc.

CHAPTER TWO: TRAINING FOR THE JOB

4. Quoted in "Interview: Shane Mielke," *Advanced Photoshop*, n.d. www.shanemielke.com.

5. Quoted in "Build Your New Career in UX Design," *Design Lab*, n.d. https://get.designlab.com.

6. Quoted in "Interview: Shane Mielke."

CHAPTER THREE: WORKING IN THE FIELD

7. Quoted in Emily Stevens, "What's a Typical Day in the Life of a Web Developer?," *Career Foundry*, September 21, 2023. https://careerfoundry.com.

8. Charlotte O'Hara, "Here's What My Typical Day Looks Like as a Web Designer/Developer," *Charlotte O'Hara*, n.d. https://www.charlotteohara.ca.

9. Quoted in "Interview: Shane Mielke."

CHAPTER FOUR: LOOKING AHEAD

10. Tom May, "The Future of Web Design," *Creative Bloq*, January 7, 2021. https://www.creativebloq.com.

FOR FURTHER RESEARCH

BOOKS

Tammy Gagne, *Become a Graphic Designer*. San Diego, CA: BrightPoint Press, 2021.

Sheryl Normandeau, *Become a Web Developer*. San Diego, CA: BrightPoint Press, 2022.

Andrew Yueh, *JavaScript Coding for Teens: A Beginner's Guide to Developing Websites and Games*. Emeryville, CA: Rockridge Press, 2022.

INTERNET SOURCES

Wanda Chung, "How to Become a Web Designer in 9 Steps and Build a Successful Career," *Hostinger Tutorials*, August 18, 2023. www.hostinger.com.

"Daily Life of a Web Designer," *Noble Desktop*, 2023. www.nobledesktop.com.

Dennis Ghyst and Kyle Mani, "Exploring the Future of Web Design: Predictions & Opportunities," *OWDT*, October 29, 2023. www.owdt.com.

WEBSITES

American Institute of Graphic Arts (AIGA)
www.aiga.org

AIGA is the oldest and largest professional organization for graphic designers. It promotes professional development through classes and seminars.

International Web Association (IWA)
www.iwanet.org

The IWA provides classes and certifications in web-related fields. It's also a source for those looking for jobs.

World Organization of Webmasters (WOW)
www.webprofessionals.org

The WOW is also known as WebProfessionals.org. It is a professional group that provides educational support to those who create, manage, and market websites.

INDEX

IMAGE CREDITS

Cover: © Frame Stock Footage/Shutterstock Images
5: © Pixel-Shot/Shutterstock Images
7: © Miljan Zivkovic/Shutterstock Images
8: © Chaosamran_Studio/Shutterstock Images
10: © Daniel Hoz/Shutterstock Images
13: © Prathankarnpap/Shutterstock Images
14: © CreateLab/Shutterstock Images
17: © Olena Yakobchuk/Shutterstock Images
18: © Song_about_summer/Shutterstock Images
21: © Tester128/Shutterstock Images
22: © Melody Smart/Shutterstock Images
25: © Impact Photography/Shutterstock Images
29: © Media_Photos/Shutterstock Images
30: © Gutesa/Shutterstock Images
32: © Rawpixel.com/Shutterstock Images
34: © Gorodenkoff/Shutterstock Images
37: © SeventyFour/Shutterstock Images
39: © BongkarnGraphic/Shutterstock Images
43: © Red Line Editorial
45: © Dragon Images/Shutterstock Images
46: © Ground Picture/Shutterstock Images
49: © McLittle Stock/Shutterstock Images
50: © photosince/Shutterstock Images
53: © PeopleImages.com-Yuri A/Shutterstock Images
56: © Andrey_Popov/Shutterstock Images

ABOUT THE AUTHOR

Kari Cornell is an award-winning children's book author who gardens, runs, and makes pottery. She lives in Minneapolis with her husband, two boys, and their sweet dog, EmmyLou.